DES Teacher Education Project
Focus Books

Series Editor: Trevor Kerry

Mixed Ability Teaching

in the early years of the secondary school

A teaching skills workbook

Trevor Kerry B.A., M.Th., M.Phil.
formerly Co-ordinator, Teacher Education Project,
University of Nottingham
Margaret Sands B.Sc., M.I.Biol.
Lecturer in Education, University of Nottingham

Macmillan Education
London and Basingstoke

First published 1982
Reprinted 1982

Published by
MACMILLAN EDUCATION LIMITED
Houndmills Basingstoke Hampshire RG21 2XS
and London
Associated companies throughout the world

Typeset by
CAMBRIAN TYPESETTERS
Farnborough Hampshire

Printed in Hong Kong

CONTENTS

INTRODUCTION

This is a workbook designed to help teachers and trainee teachers to handle mixed ability classes more effectively. It has been constructed in such a way that student teachers can engage in certain activities before, during and after classroom experience. Alternatively, experienced teachers will be able to use it either in the classroom or for study in free time. The workbook is in three parts.

Part 1 contains observation tasks, group discussion and analysis themes, and other ideas. It can most suitably be used in the early stages of training when students may be looking at videotapes, discussing classroom problems, thinking about their role as a teacher or spending a little time in school. For experienced teachers this part of the book will serve as an introduction to systematic thought about the topic.

In Part 2 there are nine tasks which may be undertaken by the user during a longer block of classroom contact. Mixed ability teaching is a recent innovation in many secondary schools, and the skills for coping with this form of classroom organisation are still evolving. The Teacher Education Project collected the views and practices of classroom teachers, heads of department and head teachers regarding methods and procedures for mixed ability teaching. In the light of this investigation a mixture of self-analysis and comment by other professionals (tutors, fellow teachers) is used to sharpen teaching skills and raise awareness of classroom practice.

Part 3 is best undertaken by students at a later stage in training when substantial classroom experience has been acquired. Practising teachers will find it useful in reviewing their own provision for mixed ability classes.

ACKNOWLEDGEMENTS

The authors wish to place on record their gratitude to the Department of Education and Science whose grant facilitated this work; and to Professor Ted Wragg, the director of the Teacher Education Project, who supported and encouraged the writing of this and our other volumes in this series. We also count it a privilege to have worked so closely with dozens of teachers and headteachers in the East Midlands.

PART 1
THINKING ABOUT MIXED ABILITY TEACHING

TOPIC 1
GOING MIXED ABILITY

A school decides to introduce some mixed ability teaching. Why? Who takes the decision? Which years become mixed ability? Which subjects?

First, *why* mixed ability? Some schools see the social benefits of mixed ability grouping as of prime importance. Integration, better personal relationships, sharing and tolerance, self-respect and confidence, co-operation, social skills, realisation of hopes and beliefs; these are all given as reasons in answer to the question: 'Why did you decide to go mixed ability?'. Other reasons revolve around solving a problem: 'sink' or 'ghetto' classes no longer exist, the less able are motivated, a fresh start can be made, there is no labelling of children, discipline is improved and morale raised. Other schools list educational reasons such as avoiding underachievement by low ability pupils or the freedom to teach in a different way[1].

The notes below give the social arguments for mixed ability as put forward to HM Inspectors when they gathered evidence which was reported in *Mixed Ability Work in Comprehensive Schools*, HMSO 1978, and the first Activity asks you to consider as many more educational arguments as you can. We return to the advantages, disadvantages, problems and benefits of mixed ability teaching in Part 3.

The arguments for mixed ability concerned with *social development,* as given to HM Inspectors[2]:

Individuals
Mixed ability grouping gives equality of opportunity to all pupils and demonstrates the equal value of each individual. It means that pupils need not be classified or put into a rank order, or feel rejected as a member of a low stream or set.

Control and relationships
Mixed ability prevents the formation of low morale often felt by bottom groups and the difficult and anti-social classes which can result. Tension between teacher and class diminishes, co-operative behaviour is restored, control and management are made easier, and relationships between teacher and taught, and among pupils become better. For the pupils, attitudes such as aggression and competitiveness become less as self-esteem and security develop.

School and society
Mixed ability encourages a sense of belonging to an unsegregated community and contributes to a non-competitive, non-élitist and undivided society, helping to counteract social class differences.

Activity 1:
Educational arguments for mixed ability

The notes above summarise arguments concerned with social development. Many of the arguments for mixed ability grouping given to the Inspectors were educational arguments. The Inspectors grouped them under the following headings:

Educational arguments on

Attitudes	Teachers and classroom methods
Expectations	Assessment
The curriculum	Pupils' work and achievement

Take each heading and write brief notes outlining the points you would expect to find there. Then refer to *Mixed Ability Work in Comprehensive Schools*, HMSO 1978, pages 17—18, to see the points which were actually made.

WHO DECIDES?

The decision to move from streaming (or banding or setting) to mixed ability may be taken by the head or by the head and staff or by groups of staff. Sometimes subject departments may decide their own policy and a school may then move (or not) to mixed ability teaching across the curriculum. In other cases head and staff of new schools, or of schools about to become comprehensive, may decide to go mixed ability and recruit new staff accordingly. An existing school may move to mixed ability by discussion and common consent. Whichever way, the head's leadership is crucial in ensuring carefully thought out aims, policy and strategies[3].

It is rare for unstreaming to take place for all years involved at the same time. More likely is that the new first years start as mixed ability classes. The decision whether or not to continue with mixed ability into the second year is taken after a few months when there has been a chance to evaluate progress. A few schools continue mixed ability into the third year. It does not often continue into the fourth and fifth year, but if it does pupils may in any case select their own examination courses which can result in streaming by choice.

WHICH SUBJECTS?

Some subjects seem to lend themselves to mixed ability grouping more than others. Art, design, RE, humanities, English, metal and woodwork, and drama are subjects where classes sometimes continue with a wide ability range beyond year three. Subjects most likely to opt out of mixed ability at an earlier time are those such as maths, languages and science, where progress depends on having mastered the previous work. Subject departments are often allowed to use their own discretion about the extent to which they adopt mixed ability teaching. It is seen, on the whole, as '*a* way' rather than '*the* way' to educate children, and a department or school must consider not only ideology but what is most suitable for the subject, the staff and the facilities.

Figures for the whole country of the number of schools which have mixed ability teaching are not easy to come by, and indeed the situation can change quite quickly. In a survey of thirty-two comprehensive schools in the East Midlands in 1977, twenty-five schools had mixed ability teaching in year one, twenty-three in year two and seventeen in year three. Fifteen schools continued some mixed ability teaching into years four and five but usually only for isolated subjects. A follow-up survey of the same schools in 1979/80 showed that, while a similar proportion of schools retained mixed ability teaching, individual schools, departments or teachers had introduced or abandoned this form of organisation.

WHAT THEN IS MIXED ABILITY?

A mixed ability class is commonly taken to be one which contains pupils representative of the whole ability range. There may be one or more children of very low, even remedial, ability as well as children of very high ability in the same class. In some schools, however, the remedial children are withdrawn from some or all lessons and taught separately until they can return to their own class. Primary schools usually have classes of mixed ability[4]

Schools which have mixed ability grouping achieve this mix in a variety of different ways: some allocate children at random to each class (but this need not necessarily result in parallel groups), some bear in mind friendship groups from primary feeder schools or the child's social background as they place children in classes, others study primary school reports on ability and achievement, or use test scores.

Activity 2:
Which subjects suit mixed ability?

Consider your own subject, its content and the teaching approach for first and second year work. Write a paragraph or two giving reasons to substantiate your view that it would (or would not) readily lend itself to mixed ability teaching.

TOPIC 2
GROUPING

The traditional type of grouping in British schools is grouping by ability. Thus a tripartite secondary school system was proposed in the 1944 Education Act to cater for the allegedly three types of children. This developed into a mainly bipartite system of grammar and secondary modern schools. On starting either type of school the children were usually further subdivided by ability, a system of grouping known as *streaming*.

COMPREHENSIVE SCHOOLS

The move towards comprehensive education aimed, amongst other things, to mirror a society in which traditional class barriers appeared to be breaking down. So we have the emergence of neighbourhood schools catering for all children from a given geographical area. However, once the pupils enter the neighbourhood comprehensive school they still have to be divided into classes. The criteria on which this is done simply represent ways of achieving intra-school grouping. Some other common methods of grouping in the comprehensive school are:

Broad banding

Broad banding is fairly wide grouping, each band containing a wider range of ability than in streaming, but not as wide as in mixed ability grouping. A nine-form entry comprehensive might decide to group pupils into three broad ability bands, each consisting of three roughly parallel classes.

Setting

In some schools children are grouped by ability, but not by general ability into A, B or C streams. Instead each subject area constructs its own rank order. So an individual pupil may be in Set 1 for English, Set 2 for French and Set 5 for mathematics.

A combination of methods

Many schools use a combination of grouping methods. A typical pattern might be for pupils to be assigned to mixed ability classes in years one and two; to be placed in bands in years three and four; and to be setted or streamed in year five.

Activity 3:
Methods of grouping

You might care now to think out, especially in the light of any experience of comprehensive schools you have had either as a pupil or a (student) teacher, the pros and cons of these methods of grouping:

(a) Random assignment to mixed ability classes
(b) Planned assignment to mixed ability classes (according to criteria such as those given above)
(c) Broad banding
(d) Setting
(e) Combination of methods

(Part 3 of this book discusses grouping in the 1980s and 1990s.)

TOPIC 3
HOW IS MIXED ABILITY TACKLED IN SCHOOLS?

TEACHING METHODS

Mixed ability grouping, of course, necessitates mixed ability teaching: techniques of teaching and of class management which suit the needs of the thirty or so individuals in the class. It is no longer possible to talk to and teach everyone at the same level because the lesson will be too difficult or too fast for some and too easy or too slow for others. Instead, a whole variety of teaching techniques have to be used judiciously, and it is a difficult task to select those which will be useful with any particular class and to balance them appropriately[5].

Teaching to the whole class will certainly form part of one's repertoire of teaching skills, but it will be used less often than with homogeneous grouping. Starting off or ending a lesson, short spells of blackboard work at an appropriate point in the lesson, or giving a lead-lesson with demonstrations and visual material to begin a topic are all occasions when whole class teaching is found to be useful. At other times of the lesson a teacher will use group work, or the children may work alone, or there may be individualised or resource-based learning independent of the teacher.

PLANNING AND PREPARATION

It follows from the section above that one's planning and advance preparation for mixed ability lessons has to be very thorough. Even before individual lessons are planned the material, skills and abilities to be taught have to be re-appraised. How much of the work previously considered suitable for homogeneous (especially grammar school) classes earns a place? Will the selected subject matter interest and motivate the whole ability range or be incomprehensible to some and too obvious to others? Can this material be dealt with in a way which relies much less on formal class teaching than before? If — for example in science — the lessons become more practical-based, does more emphasis placed on practical skills and less on theoretical manipulation fit in with the aims and objectives of the course? Do the materials and resources need a fresh look?

ASSESSMENT

The role and nature of assessment in mixed ability groups also need to be re-thought. Is marking of any sort out of place with mixed ability in that it may encourage competition? Should a pupil's attainment be assessed in relation to his own abilities and past performance or in relation to his or her position in the group? Should effort be rewarded as well as achievement? Should there be more, or less, formal assessment than with a streamed class? How are critical choices at the end of year 3 to be made?

Certainly effective assessment is necessary, not only for the child's own sake but also as one way of evaluating the changed system.

The questions posed in this section and the preceding one are questions you should ask yourself and the school staff as you teach mixed ability classes in your own teaching situation. For the next session we consider briefly how mixed ability teaching seems to be tackled in schools. Does it really answer the questions posed above, and also utilise a balance of teaching methods as outlined earlier? As you read on, compare your own mixed ability teaching with what is described. You may care to augment your reading in this area by referring to item 6 in the notes at the back of the book.

DIFFERENTIATION

In fact, mixed ability teaching is far less common in schools than mixed ability classes. A common way of teaching a mixed ability class is to teach the whole class together, aiming the lesson at the middle ability range or just below, large differences between individuals being regretfully ignored. Any individual or group work in such classes usually involves the same task for all. So the same content is taught to the whole class, the particular material used being governed by the needs of the children in the middle of the class. This means of course that pupils on either side of the middle range may not get the kind of materials or teaching best suited to them.

Her Majesty's Inspectors found that many teachers did not provide sufficient, if any, differentiation in the work for pupils of varying ability either in class teaching or individual tasks. In many cases mixed ability classes were being taught as though they were homogeneous groups, and the level of the average or just below which was provided resulted in a slow pace and underachievement. In some subjects aspects which seemed inappropriate for less able pupils or difficult to teach to a mixed ability group (in, for example, maths or French) were omitted or reduced. This picture is confirmed by research carried out by Trevor Kerry in the Sherwood Project[7].

The situation to aim at, however, is that seen in other schools where there is effective use of different teaching methods, good use of groups, and where both ends of the ability range are catered for. Aim for lessons where your pupils work at an appropriate pace and with the right materials for their level, and where individuals are taught along a carefully structured path. Plan so that the lower ability children are extended or offered a range of content or material they would not normally see and the most able have extension work of a different depth and quality.

Further teaching strategies and procedures, especially flexibility and planning, are discussed again in Part 3 of this book, making use of your own experience of teaching.

Activity 4:
Lesson planning for mixed ability

Take any topic from the first or second year work in your own subject at secondary school. Try to select a topic you will be teaching (or helping with during your school experience).

1 Produce a flow diagram to show the sequences in which you might tackle the topic with a mixed ability class. Delineate basic, essential work to be covered by all, and work which extends the topic in depth or breadth.

2 For any lesson within the sequence make out a more detailed lesson chart showing
   (a) the aim of the lesson and the work to be covered
   (b) the parts of the lesson where you would use class teaching
   (c) the activities in which the children will be engaged
   (d) the resources you would use and how you would use them
   (e) where and how you would use groups
   (f) the particular arrangements for the most and least able children.
   Discuss the plan with your tutor or fellow teacher.

3 Teach this lesson if possible, and then move on to 4.

4 Revise the plan in the light of your experience.

Refer back to this work when you tackle Focus 1 and Focus 8 in Part 2 of this book.

TOPIC 4
WORKSHEETS

GOOD WORKSHEETS

Worksheets are the most commonly used resource in mixed ability teaching. Good worksheets do a valuable job and a set which has been carefully put together can give different tasks to lead individual pupils along the right path. A good worksheet is written in sentences the pupils can understand, and thus gives clear guidance. It looks interesting to the eye and is well set out with useful and lively illustrations and good reproduction. It is challenging, offering able pupils work of a higher level and not just more of the same. It may refer pupils to other resources.

Sadly, many worksheets are not like this. They may be cluttered and unattractive. They may pose problems of understanding for the lower half of the class, and lack problem-solving activities for capable pupils.

DEATH BY A THOUSAND WORKSHEETS

Worksheets are not a panacea to solve all problems for the teacher of mixed ability classes. The use of too many worksheets or work cards can become boring, just as over-use of any other teaching method becomes tedious after a while. Used in excess they can stifle initiative, cut down on discussion, and reduce interactions[8].

Activity 5:
Worksheets

Produce a worksheet for a first year, mixed ability class, not including remedial children. It should be designed to introduce a topic, and take the the class between thirty and sixty minutes to work through. First follow the guidelines given below:

(a) *Review the topic*   — what information and understanding related to the topic do you want the pupils to acquire?

(b) *Think of possible activities*   — list as many activities as you can related to the chosen topic. A lot of ideas at this stage will help, as some will be discarded later.

(c) *Select activities*   — assuming you have more ideas than you need, select according to the following criteria:
   (i) *motivation*: is the activity going to involve the pupils? Are there things to attract both able and less able people? For how long? Suggest a time limit.

| | | (ii) | *objectives*: what other objectives, apart from the recall of facts, can be achieved through the activities? (If this question puzzles you, try reading B S Bloom, *Taxonomy of Educational Objectives*[9]; or consult your tutor.) |

(d) *Organise activities into a sequence* — can you introduce variety of activity where appropriate? How long will each take? Where in the sheet are you placing the simpler parts for the less academic pupils? How do you make clear which is additional work for those who have finished earlier sections? Consider options within the worksheet for some children.

(e) *Think about feedback* — how will you find out if your teaching is effective? Does the layout of the worksheet require the pupil to give enough responses to check on this? Is another activity required? Assessment? Homework?

(f) *Check objectives* — which activities are likely to achieve the objectives you have selected? Bearing these objectives in mind, are there any revisions you could make?

(g) *Check motivation and take a new look at the layout* — once again, is there any reason for pupils to be interested in this worksheet? Is the proposed design and layout attractive? Is the level of language simple enough for the less able pupils? Does it increase to an appropriate level in the sections for the more able pupils?

(h) *Anticipate organisation problems and safety hazards* — has your plan any special consequences for either organisation or safety?

Having considered the above sequence of eight operations, now produce your worksheet

---

FEEDBACK SESSION FOR ACTIVITY 5

When you have finished your worksheet you will find it most helpful to compare your efforts with others in small groups of four or five people. In this way you can get useful advice and criticism. Then:

1 Turn to Focus 2 in Part 2 of this book which includes *readability tests*. You may wish to do part of this exercise now. For example, you may be able to consider worksheets in use in the school where you are currently working, or do a readability test on your own worksheet.

2 Say how you would deal with a pupil who cannot either read or follow the worksheet.

TOPIC 5

GROUPS AND INDIVIDUALS

GROUP WORK

Group work is used in mixed ability teaching, especially in subjects such as science (for practical work), humanities, English, drama, craft and art. Teachers say that working in groups can help to

(a) achieve some of the social aims of mixed ability, such as co-operation, tolerance, helping and learning from each other, and

(b) ensure that different levels and pace of work are achieved.

Here we include some basic advice about handling groups. More detailed help may be sought in item 10 in the notes at the back of the book.

SKILLS NEEDED FOR GROUP WORK

1 *Decide beforehand* how your group will be made up: self selected, or selected by you, and if so on what criteria?

2 *Decide if your groups will be static* or regrouped for different activities.

3 *Have the lesson carefully prepared* and everything ready beforehand.

4 *Ensure that each group has* appropriate *subject material* and activities.

5 *Go round from group to group quickly*. Make sure you are still visible by, and still watching, other groups.

6 Don't forget to *look behind you* as you go round.

7 *Be prepared for early finishers* and have things ready for them to do.

8 *Watch for signs* that pupils are unoccupied — unnecessary movement and too much chat, incipient rowdiness.

9 Have a good way of *ending the lesson*.

INDIVIDUAL WORK

In a streamed class every child may be somewhere near the average and the teacher knows more or less what to expect from each. In a mixed ability group, teaching skills are stretched to understand and respond to the requirements of each child. *Individualised learning* is a way of dealing with thirty individuals. However, teachers sometimes speak of *individual work* as individualised learning. The individual tasks they refer to may centre on a worksheet or question sheet which is given to each child so that each is tackling the same work. This is certainly individual work but it is not individualised. In individualised learning the tasks are tailored to the needs, ability and attainment of each pupil. Independent, individualised learning, where each child is working on tasks which suit him or her, without relying on the teacher, is very rare.

Some published materials which allow individualised learning are:

1 Reid, D. and Booth, G. P., *Biology for the Individual* Books 1—9, 1970—79, Heinemann Educational Books.

2 *Schools Classics Project* materials published by the Schools Council, for young secondary school pupils.

3 In history, and to some extent in English subjects, the various titles in the *Jackdaw* kits series can be used for individual pupils.

4 *Schools Mathematics Project* textbooks (SMP) are used by some teachers to allow pupils to proceed at their own pace.

5 The *SRA Reading Laboratory* is a graded card system allowing a good deal of flexibility for individual pupils.

SLOW LEARNERS AND BRIGHT PUPILS

It is at the ends of the ability range where pupils have most need of individual attention. Pupils of *low ability* in mixed ability classes seem quite often to do better than would be expected. They are able to take part in work which is pitched a bit above them and their self-confidence may increase as teacher expectation rises. In some cases, however, teachers with inadequate knowledge of the problems of low achievers may make impossible demands, causing quite the opposite effect: a loss of confidence and a deterioration in performance.

The *most able* pupils have their problems too in mixed ability classes. They may not be stretched and quite frequently achieve much less than they could because not much is asked of them, sometimes because the teacher has no idea of what they are capable. They become frustrated and bored when time is taken up by work which is very obvious to them, or as they wait their turn for the teacher.

It is absolutely essential to plan for the slow and the bright in your mixed ability lessons. Some basic advice on how to handle them follows. In due course, however, you may wish to examine the needs of these pupils in more detail, and two more books in this series may help you (see items 11 and 12 in the notes at the back of the book).

BASIC ADVICE ON HANDLING SLOW LEARNERS IN MIXED ABILITY CLASSES

1 *Avoid dead time* which may result if they finish this work quickly even though it is not very well done. Have something else planned.
2 *Give a number of different tasks*, none very long. Concentration span is short and tasks should be clear, to the point and brief.
3 *Tell them what to do* as well as giving them written instructions. Slow learners may also be slow and *incomplete* readers.
4 *Go over key points* frequently as they have short memories.
5 *Keep interest and motivation*: arouse their curiosity, give praise, occasionally use competition.
6 *Encourage them to join in the class* even though their answers or contributions are poor compared with others.
7 *Give individual attention* when you can, either during the lesson or out of lesson hours. Keep an interest in them as people, the things they like and are good at.
8 *Be consistent in your discipline*, even-tempered but firm. Encourage success.
9 *Keep careful records* of each child's progress and of problems which need attention.

Activity 6:
Teaching bright pupils

1 In any mixed ability class with which you are working there will be children who are brighter than the others. Select one child for further observation during other lessons.
2 Write a brief case study of this child under the following headings:
   Academic performance. Include strengths and weaknesses.
   Personal interests. Record all hobbies and enthusiasms, including comments on time spent on them and levels of knowledge gained.
   Extra-curricular activities (school-based).
   Personality and relationships with other children and with staff.
   Physical description.
   Home background (briefly).

3 Compare your notes with the list given below and discuss with colleagues any general characteristics of bright pupils.
4 Make a short list of teaching points which you will wish to bear in mind when dealing with brighter pupils.

BRIGHT PUPILS: A LIST OF BEHAVIOURAL CRITERIA

(from E Ogilvie 1973, *Gifted Children in Primary Schools*, Macmillan)

1   Display of extraordinary initiative: singleness of purpose
2   Intense curiosity, sometimes in only one direction
3   Day-dreaming through boredom: possibly idle and can't be bothered with mundane tasks
4   Divergent, or even delinquent behaviour: independent
5   Highly imaginative forms of expression
6   Exasperation in the face of constraint
7   Contempt for adults of less ability: supercilious
8   Above average dependability
9   Ability to rationalise about lack of achievement
10 Highly developed sense of humour
11 Lively and stimulating conversation: not keen on writing everything down always
12 Ability to be absorbed in work for long periods
13 Suggestion of associated musical ability
14 Exceptional speed of thought
15 Exceptional depth of thought which shows itself, *inter alia*, in:
   (a) their powers to organise material
   (b) ability to see the need for many different words to express shades of meaning
   (c) their power to make and understand analysis
   (d) their power to use images
   (e) their capacity for adopting methods for unusual purposes
   (f) attention to truthful detail
16 Finding no need to labour the practical approach; jumping to the abstract
17 Finding it necessary to listen to only a very short part of the explanation given; withdraw if compelled to listen further
18 Interests — sometimes may seem unhealthy or precocious
19 Questions — may be tiresome and difficult to answer: asks lots of 'might' and 'maybe' questions
20 Bossy or cocky attitude — means of defence because they feel inferior in (say) games or handwork
21 Fear of failure — doesn't like to be proved wrong or inadequate
22 Dissatisfaction with own efforts and contempt of approval for work of standards which they realise are very ordinary
23 Perfectionism; mental speed faster than physical capabilities permit in action
24 Impatience — sometimes difficult to control — intolerant, pernickety
25 Less conformity — does not always do well; will opt out
26 Uneasy relationships with other children sometimes
27 Sensitivity and highly strung behaviour
28 Acute awareness of verbal puns etc.
29 General preference for sharing ideas with older children
30 A tendency to direct others in play and project situations
31 Alertness; often too observant for comfort
32 Good memory, frequently, but not always for 'facts' — for the way things 'work' or are related; often forgetful of 'minor' matters
33 Keenness at collecting ('rubbish' sometimes)
34 Humility about their achievements; not necessarily anxious to shine
35 Inclination, sometimes, to be self-centred or aggressive; attention-seeking
36 Lack of enthusiasm about group activities or group games
37 Appearing not to need a massive amount of sleep
38 High achievement in some line(s) or other

PART 2
CLASSROOM SKILLS WORKBOOK

INTRODUCTION

You will spend many hours teaching during your career. During this time you should work at your teaching skills like a craftsman, deliberately seeking to improve them. After qualifying, you can continue this process in your own classroom.

Part 2 of this workbook contains nine activities which focus on particular aspects of teaching skill appropriate for handling mixed ability classes. Ultimately you are responsible for developing and evaluating your own professional competence, but at the training stage you are able to call on the help of your tutor, teachers in the school and fellow students, and later upon fellow professionals.

The activities in this workbook are arranged so that you have to approach others. Do not feel threatened when these observers offer you advice. There is always a great deal to learn even if you are fortunate enough to set off with certain natural advantages. In any case it would be boring if you were commencing your career in a state of perfection with only the prospect of staying the same or becoming less professional.

The purpose behind this workbook is to provide some structure and a framework of advice within which you can develop professionally. The exercises in it are not an exhaustive account of the skills you will need for either traditional or mixed ability teaching. They are, however, basic skills which you need to acquire early in your career and to develop throughout your teaching life.

TIMETABLE

You need to organise yourself so that each of the nine focus tasks in this section of the book is completed. This is in itself a very important part of your training. Poorly organised teachers often come to grief. Do not wait for someone else to jog you into action, take the initiative yourself. Explain what is involved to the relevant observer for each task and work your way through the set. Remember to follow up in each case as suggested. When you have completed each exercise tick it off in the final column.

Focus	Topic	Who does this	When to do it	Tick when complete
1	Teaching skills	You	Week 1 first half	
2	Resources for learning	You	Week 1 second half	
3	Teaching individual pupils	You	Week 2	
4	Handling group work	You and a fellow (student) teacher	Week 3	
5	Teaching bright pupils	Your tutor	Week 4	
6	Teaching slow learners	A teacher	Week 5 first half	
7	Monitoring pupil progress	You	Week 5 second half	
8	Organising a class	Teacher or tutor	Week 6 and week 7	
9	Checking the progress of bright pupils and slow learners	You	Week 5 — week 8	

FOCUS 1
TEACHING SKILLS

WHEN TO DO THIS: During the first two and a half days of your study period.

WHO DOES THIS: You do.

WHAT TO DO: During the first day or two try to follow a class through its normal timetable to get the flavour of its school life and to see mixed ability teaching in use with a variety of subjects. The list below gives some of the skills which are thought to be important for teachers. Choose two lessons and during them make brief notes about the ways in which these skills are used. Preferably, take notes in rough first and write them up concisely on these pages later. When there is group work in progress study the teacher's interactions with the groups to examine his or her strategies under Lesson Content.

	LESSON 1 Class Subject	LESSON 2 Class Subject
Lesson organisation	Starting off the lesson	Starting off the lesson
	Explaining and giving instructions	Explaining and giving instructions
	Using whole class teaching	Using whole class teaching
	Using group work	Using group work
	Using individual work	Using individual work
	Making transitions from one activity to another	Making transitions from one activity to another
	Concluding the lesson	Concluding the lesson

Lesson content	Using appropriate language levels	Using appropriate language levels
	Selecting appropriate materials and resources	Selecting appropriate materials and resources
	Sustaining interest	Sustaining interest
	Select one group Note down all the activities going on in your selected group for a five minute period:	*Select one group* Note down all the activities going on in your selected group for a five minute period:

FOLLOW-UP

1   Talk to some of the teachers you observed about the skills you have seen them use. Try to find out why they chose to use these skills in the ways indicated.

2   Compare your notes with those of a fellow student or teacher, if possible. Discuss similarities and differences in the ways in which experienced teachers use the skills.

3   Compare similarities and differences between the two lessons which you recorded above.

READING IN SCHOOL

Ability to read well is of vital importance not only in secondary schools, but in adult life, work, and higher and further education. The reading age required in many contexts has soared in the last few years. It is no longer sufficient merely to be able to read, pupils now need such *higher reading skills* as the ability to scan and skim. They need to be able to find information rapidly via the book index or using other strategies, and to know when to slow down and read intensively.

Some newspapers need a reading age of only 8. A difficult CSE textbook may require a reading age of 16 or more to cope with it. How can these reading ages be calculated?

Below are two formulae which you can use easily. The first three hundred words and the first thirty sentences of the passage are marked, so that you can analyse the text according to the Smog and Flesch formulae described below, and see roughly what reading age you need to be able to handle this text. Will it be 10, 12, 14, 16 or 18? Make a guess first. Then read it, analyse it and see for yourself.

Books and worksheets in first year secondary science classes have a reading difficulty level two years above the ability of the average child, according to research carried out by the Schools Council, *The Effective use of Reading* project, based at Nottingham University. Levels of readability in first year texts were only marginally easier than the standard O-level course books in some subjects. History, geography and science textbooks were more difficult than those from other subjects areas, including English and mathematics.

But textbooks were not the only problem: teacher-produced worksheets were no easier to read than the published text books. Children were also asked to give their opinions on the texts. Not surprisingly, there were significant differences in what boys and girls rated as interesting or boring. The children were not specifically told the subject area each passage was from, but nevertheless the boys were generally negative towards English, and the girls towards science. The biggest disparity was in geography, which boys liked and girls found particularly boring.

Smog formula

In popular usage the term *readability* refers to aspects of a book that make it enjoyable and easy to read, but if a more objective estimate of difficulty is needed, we can turn to a readability formula. McLaughlin's Smog formula is a little rough and ready, but it is by far the quickest to work out. All you do is select three passages ten sentences long at random, and count the number of words which have three or more syllables. If we call this number p, the reading level of the passage is simply the square root of p plus eight. If you do not have a calculator handy, this can be estimated by working from the nearest perfect square to p. Thus if we counted 50 polysyllabic* words we would work from 49 (i.e. 7 x 7), and the reading level obtained would be seven plus eight, which is fifteen years.

---

*'polysyllabic' is the three-hundredth word of this passage (see *Flesch formula*)

Flesch formula

The best known American formula, that of Rudolf Flesch, may seem a little complicated, but it is in fact much more straightforward than most formulae. It requires you to work out the following sum, but not until you have counted the exact number of syllables per 100 words (NS) and average number of words per sentence (WPS) in each sample:

Reading Ease Score = 206.835 − (0.846 x NS) − (1.015 x WPS)

The following table will allow you to work out the reading level of a passage on the Flesch formula without any mindbending arithmetic. *Please note*: if you find you have detected *over* 200 syllables per 100 words in a passage — make sure you know what a syllable is!

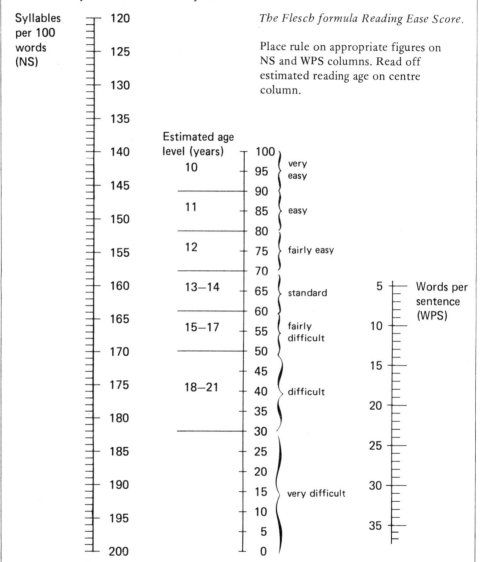

The Flesch formula Reading Ease Score.

Place rule on appropriate figures on NS and WPS columns. Read off estimated reading age on centre column.

A Practical Example

You will be working out the Smog or Flesch scores on two worksheets, but to check your arithmetic our example will be based on this section on readability.

Flesch formula: to obtain a reasonably reliable sampling, let's look at the first 300 words, and work out the average number of words per sentence and syllables per 100 words. The word 'polysyllabic' in the third paragraph is the 300th word, and leading up to it are thirteen other sentences. 'Polysyllabic' is the sixth word out of thirty, so altogether we have an average sentence length of (300 ÷ 13⅓) words, i.e. 22.7 words per sentence. On our count there are 482 syllables, which gives an average of 161 per 100 words. Using the table, this gives us a score of just below 50 — the passage is 'difficult' and certainly more than we would expect the average comprehensive school fifth-former to cope with.

Smog formula: if you just count full-stops, you reach the thirtieth one on the word 'complexity'. The number of polysyllabic words ('beginning', 'secondary', 'difficulty', 'ability', and so on) is 99. The nearest perfect square to this is 100, and the Smog level is thus $8 + \sqrt{100}$, which is 18. Again, this gives a warning — if any is needed — that this section is not easy reading.

Use formulae with caution

When using any formula it is important to remember that it is only offering information about two aspects of the text — its vocabulary and grammatical complexity.* Generally speaking long words tend to be less familiar to the reader, and long sentences more complex, but of course this is not always so. Formulae are statistical tools, and the results they give need to be treated with caution. It is sensible to regard a formula score as correct to within plus or minus one year, and the claims of publishers to have graded materials by steps of two or three months should thus be treated with suspicion. The formula is not taking account of content or conceptual difficulty, nor is it allowing for motivation, and the teacher should always remember that these can sometimes be more important than prose difficulty.

WHEN READABILITY MATTERS

Research findings indicate that there are three conditions when readability level matters most. These are:

when readers are just coming off a scheme, but do not have the breadth of reading experience to cope with unfamiliar language structures;

when motivation is low — especially therefore in certain subjects, and these may be different for boys and girls;

when the reading is unsupported — i.e. when the child is reading on his or her own without the teacher's help available.

In this connection we should recall that reference books are likely to be the most difficult books in the whole school. Why not check yours and find out?

---

* 'complexity' marks the end of the thirtieth sentence of this passage (see *Smog formula*) (These notes were compiled by Dr. Colin Harrison for the Nottingham University PGCE handbook *Schools, Teachers and Children*.)

FOCUS 2

RESOURCES FOR LEARNING

WHEN TO DO THIS: In the second half of the first week.

WHO DOES THIS: You do.

WHAT TO DO: For a couple of days in week 1 study the preparation, organisation, use and availability of teaching aids in your particular subject area. You will need to observe lessons, ask questions of teachers and watch pupils and teachers using aids and resources. Concentrate on visual or audio aids and on worksheets. Carry out the operations below.

WORKSHEETS AND WORKCARDS

Find out and note down the following information:

What kind of worksheets are used?
(are they commercially produced; produced in school, by whom, when, how; are they part of a departmental course?)

To do what jobs?
(to allow pupils to work at own speed; to cater for different abilities; to elicit written work; to set problems; to give experimental procedure; to give information?)

Readability
Carry out a readability test on two sample cards or sheets with the co-operation of the teacher concerned. Include the sheet, your calculation and results in this booklet.

21

VISUAL OR AUDIO AIDS

Collect information, by asking questions and observing, about the following:

Availability of aids (software/hardware)
(Summarise the aids available: films, slides, overhead projectors, tape-recorders, film loops and so on. Where are they located? What booking procedures apply?)

How aids are used
(Describe two lessons or parts of lessons where visual or audio aids were used; say why you think their use was effective)

ANY OTHER RESOURCES USED

Note briefly the nature and use of any other resources used in the lessons.

FOLLOW-UP

1   Talk to the teacher(s) of the lessons described above. Find out why they chose to present the lessons in audio-visual form.

2   Practise using any audiovisual or scientific equipment with which you are unfamiliar. Ask teachers or technicians to help you.

FOCUS 3

TEACHING INDIVIDUAL PUPILS

WHEN TO DO THIS: During your second and third weeks.

WHO DOES THIS: You do.

WHAT TO DO: You will have a number of opportunities to teach individual pupils. These may be pupils absent in previous lessons, bright pupils, slow learners, poor readers, or pupils with a specific difficulty in the lesson.

Study *two* children in depth while you are teaching them, by observing them in later lessons and by asking teachers about them. Complete the sections below for the two pupils after you have gathered all your information.

PUPIL 1   CONFIDENTIAL: KEEP AWAY FROM PUPIL'S VIEW

What are the child's learning problems and strengths?

Brief physical description of the child (height; weight; build; maturity)

Relationship of pupil with you (shy; friendly, precocious; able or unable to talk freely; smiling; tense; etc.)

Relationship of pupil with other pupils (well integrated; one special friend; no friends; sociometric star; friendly; introverted; etc.)

Study the child continuously for five minutes. On the grid on page 24 note every contact the child has during this time, with whom and for what purpose.

Child's language level and general ability

What did you do to help the pupil with his or her learning problem?

Have you any evidence of success or failure in your efforts to teach the pupil?

Make your own proforma for pupil 2, and study pupil 2 in the same way as you observed pupil 1.

Contact no.	With whom	Nature of contact
1		
2		
3		
4		
5		
6		
7		
8		
9		
10		

FOLLOW-UP

1 Discuss your perceptions of the chosen pupils with the class teacher or other appropriate staff. How do they differ? On what do you agree?

2 Make an opportunity to talk to these pupils again (in a lesson, in a corridor, on the games field). Do you notice any changes of attitude or behaviour towards you?

3 Look in depth at some other pupils. Make your own notes about them. Draw out similarities and differences between these individuals.

FOCUS 4
HANDLING GROUP WORK

WHEN TO DO THIS: During week 3.

WHO DOES THIS: You and a fellow student or teacher.

WHAT TO DO: Choose a lesson when it is appropriate to divide pupils into working groups, for example, when they are engaged on laboratory experiments, during group projects, or preparing a play. Ask a fellow student to study your handling of the groups by filling in the Sections A and B while watching you. You fill in the remainder.

YOUR FELLOW STUDENT FILLS THIS IN WHILE OBSERVING YOU

A   On what criteria were the pupils grouped together?

Describe the groups briefly
(number of pupils, age, sex)

Describe the groups' tasks

B   MOVING AROUND. Plot the groups on a classroom plan. For ten minutes track the teacher's movements between groups indicating how long he or she spends with each group. Try also to note the teacher's vigilance of other groups while attending to any one group.

AFTER THE LESSON fill in the following sections yourself

C   Write comments about your handling of the group work under each of
the following headings:

PREPARATION
Was everything organised before the lesson so that you were able to
concentrate on handling the groups?

MOBILITY
Were you sufficiently mobile between groups so that pupils' work was able
to proceed smoothly or was there, for example, 'dead time' while a group
waited for you?

VIGILANCE
Were you deaf and blind to all groups except the one you were with?

FOLLOW-UP

1   Discuss any difficulties you have with fellow teachers or your tutor.
Collect suggestions for future improvements.

2   Compare your responses in Section C with the record in Section B made
by the observer.

FOCUS 5

TEACHING BRIGHT PUPILS

WHEN TO DO THIS: During week 4

WHO DOES THIS: Your tutor or a fellow teacher.

WHAT TO DO: Select a bright pupil in one of the mixed ability classes you teach often. When planning lessons design special extension materials or activities which this pupil can work on. Some suggestions are given below. Arrange for your tutor or the teacher to watch the lesson in which this pupil is involved and fill in the sheet below. (You may use a group of pupils rather than an individual.)

Theme of the class's work and brief outline of the lesson:

Ways in which the student/teacher stretches the bright pupil(s):

Appropriateness of special activities or work set:

Pupil's performance at the special work or activity:

Nature of learning gains for the pupil(s):

Pupil's relationship with
(a)   peers:

(b)   the (student) teacher:

SUMMARY COMMENTS

Some suggestions for extension work for bright pupils

Let bright pupils:

(a)   do more advanced work on the same topic as the rest of the class;

(b)   research a topic related to the class work and talk about it to the class;

(c)   write the next workcard in a series;

(d)   teach two or three slower pupils a particular topic;

(e)   work alone on an extension activity such as viewing a film strip.

FOLLOW-UP

1   Talk to the child about his or her performance both encouragingly and critically.

2   Discuss your tutor's, or the teacher's, comments with him or her.

3   Think out some ways to cater for bright pupils when you teach mixed ability classes. Try to track the progress of two or three of these pupils for the rest of your teaching practice using the record sheet in Focus 9. Complete Focus 9 at the appropriate time.

FOCUS 6
TEACHING SLOW LEARNERS

WHEN TO DO THIS:	During week 5, first half.
WHO DOES THIS:	You and a fellow teacher.
WHAT TO DO:	Select a pupil with a clear learning problem such as poor reading, or low numeracy. Devise an activity which the pupil can do within a mixed ability lesson which will give extra practice in the skill which is lacking.

Nature of pupil's problem

Task devised to assist with this

TEACHER'S COMMENTS

The observing tutor or teacher should comment below about the correctness of the diagnosis of the pupil's problem, the appropriateness of the solution and whether the pupil learned anything from the experience.

Diagnosis

Appropriateness of solution

FOLLOW-UP

1   Talk to the pupil encouragingly about his or her performance in the special activity.

2   Talk to the observer about his or her comments above. Discuss how you might devise further remedial practice for this pupil.

3   Think out ways to cater for slower learners when you teach mixed ability classes. Try to track the progress of two or three of these pupils for the rest of your study period using the record sheet on Focus 9. Complete Focus 9 at the appropriate time.

Read the following before completing Focus 7.

CONFIDENTIALITY

As a teacher you will often have access to information about pupils which is of a personal nature. This information should never be communicated to anyone except those with legitimate professional reasons for knowing it. To retain confidentiality in Focus 7 use a coding system for pupils' names. Devise your own simple code.

THE CLASSIFICATION SYSTEM ON THE PROGRESS RECORD SHEET

On the record sheet on page 31 you are asked to collect information about pupil progress. Some key headings for this are supplied already. Add further headings of your own in columns E to J. Rating schemes which were used by a student teacher to complete columns B and C of this exercise and one of her extra columns are given below as examples of rating scales you might use and to illustrate the way columns E to J might be utilised.

B ATTITUDE TO LEARNING THE SUBJECT	C CLASSROOM BEHAVIOUR	E CONTRIBUTIONS TO CLASS DISCUSSIONS
1 Very unwilling	1 Disruptive	1 Silent
2 Unwilling	2 Negative	2 Diffident
3 Neutral	3 Neutral	3 Responds to direct questions
4 Enthusiastic	4 Positive	4 Contributes sensibly
5 Very enthusiastic	5 Responsive	5 Contributes often but not always sensibly

These are examples only. Make up your own classification systems and scoring methods to suit your own situation.

FOCUS 7

MONITORING PUPIL PROGRESS

WHEN TO DO THIS: During week 5, second half.

WHO DOES THIS: You do.

WHAT TO DO: Before the lesson become familiar with the record sheet on page 31. Enter your own classification system in columns E to J (see p. 29), and devise rating scales as appropriate.

Select one of the mixed ability classes which you teach often. Try to collect as much information as you can about the progress of pupils in the class. Use the record sheet provided as a guide, but add any information of your own in your own way. Imagine the purpose of the exercise is for you to be able to talk to individual parents on an Open Evening.

FOLLOW-UP

1 Discuss your completed sheet with a fellow teacher who knows the class well. To what extent do you agree or disagree in your assessments?

2 Your record sheet will probably enable you to identify some pupils who are in need of help or extra attention. Select one or two of these pupils and make suggestions for remedial action or stimuli for them.

3 Keep an eye on these pupils for the rest of this term and see how they progress.

4 Remember, one problem with writing things down is that one tends to think of them as final and unchangeable. Why not take some of your judgments and look for evidence of the *exact opposite*. Thus if you have labelled a pupil as lazy look for examples of industry by him or her. Over the next week or two try to assess to what extent your judgments are consistently valid.

NOTES

	5	4	3	2	1	Pupil Codes
						Age of pupils
A						Subject grade
B						Attitude to learning subject
C						Classroom behaviour
D						Note on any special learning strengths and weaknesses
E						
F						
G						
H						
I						
J						

and so on for rest of class

FOCUS 8
ORGANISING A CLASS

WHEN TO DO THIS: During weeks 6 and 7.

WHO DOES THIS: You, a fellow teacher or tutor.

WHAT TO DO: Select a lesson when you are teaching a mixed ability class. Fill in a preparation proforma of the kind shown here. Arrange for a fellow teacher or a tutor to watch the lesson. Ask him or her to fill in an assessment of the lesson using the headings provided in this Focus. Afterwards, discuss the lesson with the observer.

TEACHER'S COMMENT SHEET

1 What are the overall aims and the aims for the lesson?

2 What teaching methods are being employed? How effectively?

3 Is the content of the lesson suitable for the age and ability of the pupils?

4 What aids and resources are being used? How effectively?

5 Is classroom organisation effective?

6 Note those pupils who are involved and those who are not. Suggest why in each case.

7 Overview of effectiveness of lesson.

8 Points to concentrate on putting right.

9 Particular strengths.

FOLLOW-UP

1 Compare your preparation sheet with the tutor's or teacher's comment sheet.

2 Discuss any differences which emerge between the two accounts of the lesson and try to explain them.

3 Decide on any actions necessary to improve your teaching next time.

OBJECTIVES:

SUBJECT CONTENT	WORK TO BE COVERED: PROCEDURES AND ACTIVITIES		TIME ALLOWED	RESOURCES NEEDED	ACTION RE BRIGHT AND LESS ABLE PUPILS
	What you do	What the pupils do			

If possible, before discussing the lesson with the observer or tutor add your own summary comments here:

Did the children learn anything? How do you know?

Assess your own performance during the lesson.

FOCUS 9
CHECKING THE PROGRESS OF BRIGHT PUPILS AND SLOW LEARNERS

WHEN TO DO THIS: Continuously, after weeks 4 and 5, Focus 5 and 6.

WHO DOES THIS: You do.

WHAT TO DO: In Focus 5 and 6 you are asked to keep records on up to three bright pupils and up to three slow learners from week 5 until the end of teaching practice. For each of these selected pupils use a record sheet of the kind provided here. At the end of the practice review the progress of these pupils.

BP1

Age

General ability

Reading age (if you can discover this)

Maths grade (if you can discover this)

Grade for your subject

Attitude to learning your subject

Classroom behaviour

Comments about the specific needs of the pupil

How did you try to meet these specific needs?

How successful were you?

FOLLOW-UP

Review your teaching strategies, successes and failures with these pupils. Suggest below what you have learned about slow learners and bright pupils which will help you in your future handling of these pupils.

PART 3
REFLECTIONS ON EXPERIENCE

The skill of mixed ability teaching is an *advanced* teaching skill. In other words, to teach a mixed ability class effectively the practitioner needs to possess already several basic skills (the abilities to cope with whole class teaching, with group work and individualised learning, for example) and to combine these into a unified teaching process. This booklet has, in Parts 1 and 2, been directed towards the acquisition of the sub-skills and their combination into an appropriate whole.

In the aftermath of your experience on teaching practice or as a full-time teacher you should now be able to bring together some insights from your experience in order to explore more fully the concept and process of mixed ability teaching.

TOPIC A
EXAMINING THE UNDERLYING PHILOSOPHY

ADVANTAGES AND DISADVANTAGES OF MIXED ABILITY TEACHING

What are the reasons which have persuaded many educationists that a mixed ability organisation is to be preferred to other possible groupings for education?

In a piece of research carried out by the Teacher Education Project we asked teachers what were the advantages and the disadvantages of mixed ability teaching for pupils in comprehensive schools. What follows is a summary of their opinions:

ADVANTAGES OF MIXED ABILITY TEACHING	
1 Children are not labelled: no pupil feels superior or inferior.	
2 There is an improved 'class atmosphere' because of 1.	
3 Discipline problems are fewer since there are no 'ghettos'.	
4 Pupils learn to work co-operatively.	
5 There are more opportunities for teacher-pupil contacts.	
6 There are more, and more meaningful, pupil-pupil contacts.	
7 Late developers are given improved chances.	
8 Pupils may, more readily, work at their own level.	
9 A levelling up of attainment occurs (slower pupils improve their performance).	
10 There is improved language development.	
11 Brighter pupils can help less able ones.	
12 Pupils can delay decisions about specialism.	
13 There is more time given to individual pupils.	
14 There is more time available before pupils' abilities need to be assessed.	
15 All pupils appear more confident.	
16 There is less stress or emotional tension than in a streamed situation.	

Activity 7:
Advantages of mixed
ability teaching

Look through the list of sixteen advantages of mixed ability teaching given on page 35. In the blank space beside each item make your own comments. Particularly note whether or not the suggested advantage has been apparent in the mixed ability classes which you have met.

Activity 8:
Disadvantages of mixed
ability teaching

Before proceeding to look at what experienced teachers saw as disadvantages of a mixed ability organisation, from your own experience jot down here what YOU think are disadvantages or problems.

1

2

3

4

5

6

When you have completed this, compare your list with the one which follows.

PROBLEMS OF MIXED ABILITY TEACHING

(as seen by experienced teachers)

1 Appropriate teaching materials are sometimes lacking.
2 It is hard to pitch a whole-class lesson at the correct level.
3 Cliques develop among pupils.
4 Pupils still choose friends from their own social class and intelligence level.
5 It is difficult to keep track of all pupils' progress.
6 Teachers need to be committed to the philosophy of mixed ability teaching.
7 Teachers need to spend a vast amount of time in preparation and resource-making.
8 Bright pupils waste a lot of time.
9 Teachers spend time disproportionately on the slow learners.
10 Slow learners learn that they always fail.

EXAMINING THE SOCIAL BENEFITS

In a recent HMI report the opinion was expressed that, while teachers often talk about the social aims and benefits of mixed ability teaching, they are not usually able to articulate what these aims and benefits are.

Activity 9:
Social benefits of mixed
ability teaching

In the light of your experience of mixed ability teaching can you list any social aims or benefits peculiar to this kind of grouping?

For further study

Two contrasting accounts of the viability of mixed ability teaching are given in Sands and Kerry, 1982, *Mixed Ability Teaching*, Croom Helm. They are Tom King's chapter 'Mixed ability and the community school ideal' and Frank Collier's 'A retreat from mixed ability teaching'.

THE MINIMUM REQUIREMENTS FOR SUCCESS?

When the Schools Council investigated mixed ability teaching in mathematics it found that schools having successful mixed ability teaching tended to be supported by a cluster of circumstances which helped this form of organisation to flourish. These circumstances included:

1 A supportive headteacher.
2 An established school.
3 An able head of department.
4 Smallish classes.
5 No lack of financial support.
6 Good accommodation.
7 Good reprographic facilities.
8 Few disruptive pupils.
9 Remedial withdrawal system.
10 'Float teachers' to cope with slower pupils.

For further study

Schools Council, 1977, *Mixed ability teaching in mathematics,* Evans Methuen Educational. Ingleson, S., 'Creating conditions for success with mixed ability classes' in Sands and Kerry, 1982, *Mixed Ability Teaching,* Croom Helm

WHAT KIND OF TEACHER?

In the Teacher Education Project's research the teachers who were interviewed and watched at work with mixed ability classes suggested a certain profile of a teacher of mixed ability classes.

PROFILE OF A TEACHER

A teacher of mixed ability classes should
 . . . prepare lessons thoroughly

 . . . not be too dominant

 . . . be *au fait* with and value the subject-matter of lessons

 . . . ask leading questions

 . . . be aware of social groupings within the class

 . . . be a good organiser

 . . . know how to use feed-back from pupils

 . . . be able to devise resources and workcards

 . . . try new methods of teaching and take risks

 . . . admit mistakes and learn from them

 . . . know what standards can reasonably be expected from pupils

 . . . be able to describe and cope with exceptional pupils

 . . . be able to analyse teaching objectives

 . . . accept each pupil as an individual

**Activity 10:
Teaching profile:
additional skills**

Look critically at the Profile of a Teacher above. Are there any teaching skills you would want to add to the list given there? If so, jot them down.

GROUPING IN THE 1980s AND 1990s

Our review of criteria for grouping in Part I was by no means complete, and it may be productive to speculate on some possible ways of grouping pupils which have not, as yet, been put to the test in the education system. Below are two suggestions, and you may be able to add to these.

Matching teacher–pupil personalities

Very little work has been done in the field of matching pupil personalities to teaching personalities. Thus, do retiring introverted pupils learn better with rather low-profile introvert teachers or with forceful, extrovert ones? To what extent does personality affect the learning process? Although more research needs to be done before we can begin to answer these questions it is conceivable that placement of pupils in classes *could* be done by compatibility of personality between the teacher and the taught.

Preferred learning style

There is some evidence to suggest that able pupils prefer, and learn better as a result of, rather formal or traditional teaching methods — teacher-directed instruction and written work in preference to self-directed activity. Should the teaching style of individual teachers be matched to the preferred learning style of pupils? Again, more research is necessary before extravagant claims can be made for adopting this criterion for grouping.

Both of these suggested criteria deserve as serious consideration as was once given to the debate about single-sex or co-educational schools. No doubt there are other methods of grouping which would be equally worthy of attention.

Activity 11:
Grouping in the 1980s and 1990s

Can you suggest any other criteria for grouping, other than those already listed in this book, which might be worthy of consideration in the future? If so, jot them down, with a brief rationale explaining why you think the criterion is important.

TOPIC B

SOME REFLECTIONS ON TEACHING STRATEGIES AND PROCEDURES

'FLEXIBLE' TEACHING

Earlier in this booklet (page 37) we asked what kind of teacher was necessary for successful exploitation of a mixed ability organisation. Some responses given by experienced and effective practitioners were listed. It was clear from our research that one overriding concept coloured the views of our sample about this question. That concept was 'flexibility'.

What did our respondents mean by a 'flexible' approach to teaching? As already hinted, the successful, and flexible, teacher of mixed ability classes was one who brought a *range* of teaching skills to bear upon each lesson. But there was more to it than that.

In the first place, flexibility extended to attitudes. It suggested awareness of the differing needs, aptitudes and personal qualities of individual pupils. It had a social flavour in that flexible teachers were characterised as encouraging pupils to think and act independently.

Skills featured strongly in the concept. Flexible teachers were those who used a variety of teaching methods: of these, the three teaching modes of whole class and group teaching and individualised learning, were pre-requisite.

But such teachers also varied the content, style and pace of lessons: teacher exposition, pupils' use of resource materials, teaching from television and film, and learning through discussion were all aspects of varied and flexible teaching.

The social dynamics of the classroom, too, could be handled sympathetically by teachers with a flexible approach. Children may be grouped within the classroom by friendship, shared work interests or other unstable criteria. Flexible teachers were sensitive to the need to change groupings to suit the situation.

Resource-based learning is becoming increasingly common. Flexible teachers could make use of a wide variety of resources: text books, worksheets, audiovisual equipment of every kind, the blackboard, commercial kits and self-assembled collections.

In mixed ability teaching it is frequently the case that pupils are working individually on different topics and at very different cognitive levels. Flexible teachers could handle these multifarious activities, and were able to discern how much time to give to any one topic and recognise the psychological moment to progress to new work.

Ability to work with colleagues, specifically in a team-teaching situation or as part of a large department, was clearly a component of flexible teaching.

Of course, all the skills indicated so far are important skills for teachers in any kind of organisation, whether it be mixed ability, streamed, or built upon other criteria. However, the need for these skills is highlighted with the kind of relatively informal teaching styles demanded by mixed ability classes. Some description of mixed ability lessons in progress are given in Trevor Kerry's chapter 'Mixed ability teaching in the humanities' and in Mervyn Flecknoe's 'Mixed ability teaching in science' in Sands and Kerry (1982).

For the remainder of this workbook we are going to isolate and discuss just a few of these skills, the possession of which seem to be crucial to effective mixed ability teaching.

PLANNING FOR MIXED ABILITY TEACHING

Planning is not synonymous with preparation (i.e. lesson preparation). Indeed planning is multi-dimensional. It involves

. . . planning for mixed ability organisation at school and departmental levels

    formulation of global aims and objectives of education

    school level debate on the desirability of adopting a mixed ability organisation

    school level decision-making on procedure and administration

    departmental discussions on the implications of adopting a mixed ability organisation

    departmental decisions on procedures and administration.

. . . planning for pupils at departmental level

    formulation of curriculum aims and objectives

    discussions and decisions about
        (a) curriculum content   (b) teaching methods
        (c) how to track pupil progress   (d) resources
        (e) review and evaluation of procedures and curriculum

. . . planning for lessons at classroom level

formulation of immediate aims and objectives

specific preparation for individual lessons:
the content
how to put the material across
specific activities for exceptional pupils
resources required
what the pupils should know at the end of the lesson
how to test what has been learned

The chances are that you will not have been involved in the first of these items, planning for mixed ability organisation at school level. However, as a teacher or student teacher you will have experienced planning at both departmental level and at classroom level. In Part 1 you practised planning for individual lessons. In the following activity you are asked to look at planning on the departmental level.

Activity 12:
Planning for pupils at
departmental level

1 Over the last term or so you have worked as a member of a subject department. Review the thinking and provision of your department about mixed ability teaching. A number of sub-headings are provided to help you analyse the departmental provisions.

2 Next to your review of provisions write a short critique explaining why the provisions are (or are not) successful in your view. Jot down the reasons for your answers.

(a) *aims and objectives*
Provision: Critique:

(b) *curriculum content*
Provision: Critique:

(c) *teaching methods*
Provision: Critique:

(d) *tracking pupils' progress*
Provision: Critique:

(e) *resources*
Provision: Critique:

COPING WITH EXCEPTIONAL PUPILS

Detailed strategies and suggestions for dealing with bright pupils and slow learners are to be found in other Focus workbooks in this series. The aim of this section is to point to some *common problems* which teachers face when confronted by slow learners or bright pupils in mixed ability classes. The causes of the problems are, of course, quite different in the case of bright pupils on the one hand and slow learners on the other.

Throughout the Project's research into exceptional pupils in mixed ability classes teachers talked about these pupils as exhibiting common problems. They were . . .

. . . dead time

This is the time between a pupil finishing one activity and starting another. Bright pupils complete work quickly because tasks are often too easy for them. Slower pupils can often manage only a sentence or two, and then they feel they have exhausted the topic.

. . . boredom

This may result from spending too much time waiting for the teacher to correct work, approve progress to the next step or take remedial action.

. . . lack of motivation

Children who are often unoccupied and bored can easily lose interest.

. . . disruption

The creative mind continually seeks new diversions. The less able may simply be looking for something more relevant to do! The bored pupil is always a potential trouble-maker.

. . . provision of special work

The previous four problems imply that the teacher must of necessity provide special work for pupils at both ends of the ability spectrum.

. . . increased preparation time by the teacher

Implicitly, providing special work means spending more time in preparing lessons.

. . . linguistic and cognitive levels of worksheets and texts

One perennial problem of mixed ability classes is that teachers tend to 'teach to the middle'. Part of the 'special provision' for exceptional pupils is to cater for bright pupils who need to be stretched intellectually and to cope with slow learners for whom the language of text or instructions may not be clear.

. . . emotional and pastoral problems

Finally, both sets of pupils may (but not necessarily) have problems of a social nature, e.g. concerning peer-group relations. Bright pupils are sometimes rejected as 'teacher's pet', and slower learners are labelled 'thick'. The teacher needs to bear relationship problems in mind when organising classroom work and activities.

SELF-TEACHING

One way in which problems arising from the needs of exceptional pupils can be reduced is to make the pupils more independent. For example, a bright child may need to be allowed to check his own answers against the answer book, or to decide whether to proceed to the next exercise, or to plan the direction of his next piece of work (subject to teacher approval). For a slow learner it may be helpful to tape-record rather than write instructions or to allow him to augment written work with photographs, tapes or other non-written work.

**Activity 13:
Coping with exceptional pupils**

We have listed some ways in which pupils can become LESS dependent on the teacher. Devise some strategies of your own for making pupils less dependent on the teacher. If possible, try them out and comment on their effectiveness.

TEAM-TEACHING

As part of the Teacher Education Project's survey of mixed ability teaching in local schools, headteachers and teachers were asked to list training procedures likely to be helpful to students and probationers. It was commonly suggested that young teachers should experience team-teaching as part of their basic training. Team-teaching involves an important sub-set of skills which are summarised below.

SOME TEAM-TEACHING SKILLS AND QUALITIES

1 Ability to plan work co-operatively
2 Ability to formulate longer-term aims and objectives
3 Readiness to pool ideas and skills
4 Willingness to put one's own teaching on view
5 Capacity to share equipment or work-space
6 Willingness to accept advice, criticism from colleagues
7 Openness to curriculum change
8 Skills of careful administration and record-keeping

RECORD KEEPING

In Part 2 of this workbook we suggested a proforma for collecting information about pupils' progress. Keeping track of this progress is one of the most vital skills of a teacher in a mixed ability class because the children will be at vastly different stages of educational, cognitive and emotional development. Information can be collected in many different ways and can cover different aspects of the child's development. Here are just some pieces of information which might be worth keeping in whatever records you keep, and some ways of recording that information:

(All records should preserve confidentiality.)
1 A written profile of the pupil, added to and revised regularly.
2 A list of subject grades, marks or comments.
3 Records of formal test results (IQ, VRQ, Reading Age, etc).
4 Photocopies of unusually good/bad/creative work or examples showing the child's special difficulties.
5 Comments on skills specific to the subject.
6 Analyses of specific difficulties or strengths of given pupils.
7 Reminders to oneself about work or procedures to try out with specific pupils.

8 Child-studies of one or two pupils (to practise one's own analytical abilities).
9 Background information affecting the pupil's ability to learn.
10 Copies of comments made about pupils on the termly or annual reports.
11 Periodic analysis of each child's progress.

Activity 14:
Record keeping

Using the ideas on the previous page, and any of your own, devise your own tailor-made record-keeping scheme for tracking the progress of your pupils.

HANDLING RESOURCES

Mixed ability teaching is often more resource-based than other teaching styles: children progressing at different rates must be less dependent on the teacher and more dependent upon facilities available in the classroom. In Part 2 of the workbook you looked generally at the resources available in your subject department. In the light of your experience of these you might like to pursue the question of resource provision in your school more closely.

In the following activity you are asked to reflect on the resource provision of your teaching practice or current school and to answer a number of questions about it. Write a sentence or two to elaborate or illustrate your answer in each case.

Activity 15:
Handling resources

1 *Who selected* the resources in the departmental or school resource collection?

2 How was the *quality* of the resource items (slides, tapes, charts) monitored?

3 Was there an adequate *quantity* of resource materials available?

4 Where were resource materials *located*? Were they easily accessible?

5 How were they *indexed* or classified?

6   Was the range of resource materials adequate to cover *all ages and abilities*?

7   Was the range of resource items adequate to meet your *curriculum needs*?

8   How were *new materials* added to up-date the collection?

9   Were you able to handle the appropriate *audiovisual equipment* necessary to teach using resource-based learning?

10 Were pupils able to *study privately* using items from the resource collections as they would use library books?

11 Were adequate facilities available to enable you to make *'home-produced'* resource items?

12 What procedures were there within the school or department for monitoring the *quality* of 'home-produced' resource materials?

13 In the light of experience how would you set out to improve your own *use of resources* in your teaching?

NOTES

1 Dooley, P., Kerry, T. and Smith, A., 1977, *Teaching Mixed Ability Classes*, School of Education publication, Nottingham University.
2 HMI Series: Matters for discussion 6, 1978, *Mixed Ability Work in Comprehensive Schools*, HMSO.
3 Bastiani, J., 'The Role of the Subject Department' in Kerry, T. (ed.), 1978, *Reports of work in progress*, Occasional Paper 2, the Teacher Education Project, Nottingham University.
4 Ridley, K. 'Mixed ability teaching in the Primary School' in Sands, M.K., and Kerry, T. 1982, *Mixed Ability Teaching*, Croom Helm.
5 Wragg, E. C., (ed) 1976, *Teaching Mixed Ability Groups*, David & Charles.
6 Sands, M. K. 'Teaching methods: myth and reality' in Sands, M.K., and Kerry, T., 1982, *Mixed Ability Teaching*, Croom Helm.
7 Kerry, T. 'The demands made on pupils' thinking in mixed ability classes' in Sands and Kerry (1982).
8 Wragg, E.C., 1978, 'Death by a thousand worksheets', TES.
9 Bloom, B.S., 1956, *Taxonomy of Educational Objectives*, Longmans.
10 Kerry, T. and Sands, M. K. 1982, *Handling Classroom Groups*, Macmillan Education.
11 Kerry, T., 1982, *Teaching Bright Pupils in Mixed Ability Classes*, Macmillan Education.
12 Bell, P. & Kerry, T., 1982, *Teaching Slow Learners*, Macmillan Education.

FURTHER READING

Books

Barker-Lunn, J.C., 1970, *Streaming in the Primary School*, NFER. Research report of a massive study involving 2,000 schools.
Davies, B. and Cave, G., 1977, *Mixed Ability Teaching in the Secondary School*, Ward Lock. A series of papers including descriptions of 'going mixed ability' in two secondary schools.
Davies, R.P., 1975, *Mixed Ability Grouping*, Temple Smith. Looks at five curriculum areas (History, English, French, Maths and Science) as well as more general issues.
Ferri, E., 1971, *Streaming: two years later*, NFER. A follow-up study to Barker-Lunn's research.
Jackson, B., 1964, *Streaming*, Routledge. A survey of streaming through the eyes of schools, teachers and parents.
Kelly, A.V., 1974, *Teaching Mixed Ability Classes*, Harper Row. Some practical ideas with missionary flavour.
Newbold, P., 1978, *The Banbury Report*, NFER. A comparative study of streams and mixed ability organisation in one school.
Postlethwaite, K. and Denton, C., 1978, *Streams for the Future*, Pubansco. Further details about the Banbury Enquiry.
Sands, M.K. and Kerry, T., 1982, *Mixed Ability Teaching*, Croom Helm.
Wragg, E.C. (ed), 1976, *Teaching Mixed Ability Groups*, David & Charles. Covers work in seven curriculum areas, along with ideas of general application to mixed ability classes.

The following journals may be useful in whole or part:

Cambridge Journal of Education, vol. 6, 15–23, 1976.
Forum 20, 2 (1978)
Forum 21, 3 (1979)

NOTES